ALSO BY OMAR MUSA

BOOKS

Millefiori	(Penguin, 2018)
Here Come The Dogs	(Hamish Hamilton, 2014)
Parang	(Penguin, 2013)
The Clocks	(Muse Arts Magazine, 2010)

PLAYS

Since Ali Died	(2018)

ALBUMS

Since Ali Died	(2017)
DEAD CENTRE	(2016)
MoneyKat	(2012)
World Goes to Pieces	(2010)
Massive EP	(2009)

Omar Musa is an award-winning Bornean-Australian author, poet, rapper and visual artist from Queanbeyan, Australia. His debut novel "Here Come the Dogs" was long-listed for the International Dublin Literary Award and Miles Franklin Award and he was named one of the Sydney Morning Herald's Young Novelists of the Year in 2015. He has performed at venues such as the Brixton Academy and Brooklyn Academy of Music, and received a standing ovation at TEDx Sydney at the Sydney Opera House. His one-man play, "Since Ali Died", won Best Cabaret Show at the Sydney Theatre Awards in 2018. He has had several solo exhibitions of his woodcut prints.

LIZZY,
Hope to meet you again at the
LEFT LION! Yours in poetry
& semangat — spirit.
OMAR

KILLERNOVA

OMAR MUSA

NOTTINGHAM,
2022

Broken Sleep Books

lay out your unrest

*Dedicated to
Aerick LostControl,
Yee I-Lann,
Tamparuli Living Arts Centre
and Pangrok Sulap*

In memory of Salleh Ben Joned

'My blood was full of them; my brain bred islands'

ELIZABETH BISHOP

A NOTE ON WOOD

Borneo, shared by Malaysia, Indonesia, and Brunei, was once the most densely forested island in the world. The people of this island have always carved wood beautifully. The seafaring people of the north-eastern coastline (like my biological grandfather's people, the Suluk) carved floral designs and dragons into the prows of shoreline lepa boats and high sea karakuas, just as the peoples of the interior of the island carved animal spirits into the beams of longhouses or whittled figures into the handles of mandaus, used to take heads in war. My grandmother's people, the Kedayan, carved their grave markers with belian – ironwood. When ironwood is cut, it goes from bright yellow to almost black, and it emanates a lemon scent that many Dayak (Indigenous) people say guards against tigers and elephants. It is now an endangered species.

My uncle Bakri would come home from working on a palm-oil plantation in Lahad Datu (many species of tree replaced by one, but that's a different story) and weave rattan and carve wood. When I was a child, living in Australia, he would send me hand-carved toys and woven rattan bags. He was self-taught; it always amazed us how naturally these skills came to him. Even now that he's retired, he carves miniature boats from jackfruit wood — Sama-Bajau lepa-lepa and Bugis pinisi, a nod to his people, the greatest seafarers in South-East Asia. He uses chopsticks as masts and scraps of curtain for the sails.

They say Hang Tuah, the famous Malay warrior, was a carver of wood. Abdul Rahman-Abdullah, the Malay-Australian wood sculptor, makes large works that in his own words, reach "behind the Islamic veneer of our traditions, back to an animist relationship with the world." He uses Jelutong, a Malaysian hardwood.

I carve cheap MDF. It's compressed sawdust— a by-product of the corrupt logging industry — not the smooth, hard cherry wood used by the Japanese woodcut masters. MDF carves easily and you don't need expensive tools. It's what I was taught on. It's held together by carcinogenic glue, hazardous to the lungs, and is illegal in some countries. It is a distant, bitterly ironic echo of my ancestors, but a concession I have been willing to make to chase that connection.

Having been born and growing up far away from Borneo, in Australia, it would have felt false to use traditional motifs. Instead, I made my own iconography, a jumble of cartoons, emoticons and pop-culture references mixed with images of the natural world – turtles, sacred hornbills, leopards. I carve my stories in wood. My ancestors sailed in wood. They will carry me out in wood.

I'd be remiss if I didn't mention the people who got me into this. I have been, for many years, a huge fan of the Bornean punk rock and woodcut collective Pangrok Sulap ("Pangrok" is the Malayanisation of "punk rock," a "sulap" is a farmer's resting hut in the Kadazan-Dusun language). Their large-scale works, often with an activist bent relating to Bornean identity, government corruption, self-sufficiency or protecting the environment, really appealed to me. We orbited each other without meeting for a long time.

In 2018, I sailed up the mighty Mahakam River (on the Indonesian side of Borneo) by public ferry, sleeping on the deck, not speaking English, making brief new friendships as I travelled to the heart of the island. I was burnt out, trying to get my head straight. Depression, self-doubt, and years of touring had taken its toll. I had lost the love for writing and performing. But being at the heart of the island, sometimes travelling by foot through the forest, seeing the ancient longhouses and getting by on the kindness of strangers (who were yet so familiar) was a transformative experience. I realised I was looking for a new way to express myself. But what? I certainly didn't expect it would be something in the visual arts.

But now that I look back, maybe the many wood carvings I saw on that trip, sub-consciously put the idea in my head. One encounter, in particular, I never forgot. Pak Jayau, an elderly Dayak Benuaq man, saw me lost on the side of the road and beckoned me into his house, every railing, eave, and beam of which he had built and carved himself, despite being doubled over with age. In the beams he had carved women giving birth to snakes, men with snakes coming out of their mouths. These were things he had dreamed, he said. He even put on a necklace made of carved wooden talismans that he said had protective powers. He told me that he had built the house to teach young people about Dayak culture, which he felt was rapidly being lost.

At times, on the river, I felt a soulful, mystical connection to my homeland. At times, I felt like a fraud. At times, a tourist. At other times, reading old accounts of Borneo from the 1920s, to help me understand the land through which I travelled, I had the unnerving feeling of looking at my homeland through the lens of a colonial anthropologist.

Several weeks later, I was performing at the Tamparuli Living Arts Centre, back in Malaysian Borneo. I saw that Aerick LostControl – a heavily tattooed, scarred punk rocker, activist, and loosely-affiliated member of Pangrok Sulap – was running a woodcarving workshop. I hesitantly asked him if I could join, and he welcomed me with his patented, massive, maniacal grin. Sitting on the earth, he taught me how to cut my designs into the wood with a U or V shaped gouge, then roll it with ink and press it to the paper or cloth. We did that last part by stamping on it with our feet or even dancing on it while playing music, to imbue the artwork with more semangat – spirit. Pressing the prints using your feet is a very South-East Asian way of doing it, and something Borneans learned from the great Indonesian collective Taring Padi, although I have heard of people in Cambodia doing it this way as well. The first thing I carved was the most beautiful thing I knew, although I had never seen one: a Bornean clouded leopard. If I made a mistake while carving, it was done. Writing letters backwards (because the woodblocks print in mirror image), was a constant source of early mistakes. There were ways of covering it up, but really you just had to move on. The wood was unforgiving in that way. But it was fun, I could be playful again, and return to the spirit that first moved me as a child, drawing with my Aussie grandma, or scribbling down my thoughts in poetry form. For what felt like the first time in years, I made something from a place of joy. I was immediately addicted.

I have since met all the members of Pangrok Sulap. They have sat with me and given me heaps of encouragement and semangat. In Australia, there were people instrumental in helping me with my prints, and encouraging me with my art, principally Clare Jackson, Rinaldo Hartanto, and Tim Pauszek at Megalo Print Studio in Canberra, as well as my friends Abdul Abdullah and Jason Phu.

In a time when we cannot travel, windows and mirrors become portals to strange reveries and memories. We all deal with our own killernovas. The ripples from the massive events in our histories — colonisation, family trauma, heartbreak — wash up on our shores today. Traversing fire-ravaged Australia, Bornean rainforests and coral reefs, and COVID cabin fever dreams, this is my deadly playful exploration of family and flags, bodies and borders, environmental destruction, writing, addiction, and recovery. As they say in the Suluk language, layag sug — let's sail together!

OMAR MUSA

ISLANDS

Seismic upheaval
beneath the page's glass skin.

Syllables bubble up — mistakes
made of magma, they become muscled

with mineral and moment, fern, fluorescent
flowers that lead down to the shore,

reflecting the coral that blooms and wanes
beneath the waves, the jellyfish blue pulse. Time

anneals the page into a mirror, but the right temperature
can create fierce clarity, deep down to the bottom.

Sweep out the circular net,
reticello pattern of shadow —

comb the seagrasses and algae at low tide
for squid, shrimp and the

songs of lost sailors.

THE OFFERING

FOR BHENJI

bodies
and water.

bodies
of water.

seven thousand

Bodies
in water —

maintain posture,

bent forward in reverence, torsos to sun,
shoulders cliffs and eyes downcast,
demure — no, playful — forever, palm leaves
flutter-flit like lashes, somatic temples
conceived from volcanic ash, this
movement mirrors migratory birds,
the thin topaz horizon dimming now to *night*,

tonight,

maintain posture,

the faster the beat, the slower the movement,

twist wrists inward and outward
with winds and tides,
form hands from sand and rock,
your promontories and bays will

      hold bones,
      hold docks,
      hold call to prayer,

hold steady the torch that blades across the face of the deep,
waves hip-toss beneath woven sheets — purple & garnet,
mulberry & mangosteen peel — in this dyeing light,
the sarong is a sail — tie it to an upright oar and speak
life into the vessel, these decks were divined for dancing,
run hands along the blood-spilt grain, worn by soles,
salt-worn, warn of plague, dying kisses and childbirth —

    for what it's worth,

we have been here many times already,
you know it well already (the jubilant fear, distilled tears),
now brass fingernails tremble to read ripples,

      read tides,
      read throat,
      read nipples,

read steaming broth and salted fish with butterfly tongue,
vocabulary palls then shreds in vapour,
    think sanskrit,

think dancers,
choreographed in collaboration with the waves,
now melt the stars down to a single golden ingot,
wear it on a chain of islands

    forever more

it will light your faces —

    the privileged, the hateful, the hurtful,

        the stateless.

the refuse of the world has atomised,
ancestral seas a great gyre of plastic,
    rising,
blood pressure in the giant's corrupted body,
you see, duterte is killing addicts in the street
and the new malaysia is the same as the old.

yet still.

fish scales turn alabaster on the belly of the moon,
we remain seraphim with fishermen's hands —
    capitalist christians, muslim animists —
dried blood between thumb and forefinger,
configured together to point a way forward,

for we are all trilingual not so deep down —

      speak god,
      speak flesh,
      speak ocean

speak up, martial your arts,
pivot, twist, bend back like a bow,
stay flexible as borderline,
stay   controlled

because if your limbs, in patterns, seamlessly unfold,

      the dance, the dance, the dance

      will never die.

maintain posture.

the faster the beat, the slower the movement.

we make an offering tonight   to you.

this   here   is our offering.

SEA SILK

The last woman in the world who knows how to spin sea silk lives in
Sardinia. Byssus mussels, four fish long, cling to the seabed by beard,
secreted threads of silken saliva; 100 dives for 30 grams. Harvest it,
preen it, soak it in a secret brew of spices — the result is so fine a pair of
gloves can be folded up to fit into half a walnut shell. The woman sings
into the spices: the cloth then illumes like gold. Plastic and Shell petrol
are choking the mussels to death, these molluscs spoken of in the Bible,
described by ancient Chinese wayfarers. Dive deep for the song of the
ocean, says the woman. It cannot be bought, only gifted.

*

In Semporna, I've met Sama boys
who compression dive for pearls or
to fish-scare skipjack into nets —
they clamp their mouths over green garden hose
and dive down through a strata of blue on
dark blue, bubble-clad, sons and fathers and
uncles, the pressure on their skinny frames
so heavy they chance death.

Laughter over a cigarette.
A simple broth must do.

The hose, it glows, chugs diesel-tainted
breath from surface to poverty of light.
The bends swell joints to madness.

Their hair, it sways,
black as silt, as sable,
each fibre so delicate
it brushes the water
but leaves no mark.

They did not tell me if they heard any song.

WERELEOPARD

You have waited your
whole life for this —
ever since land bridges
melted, the seas rose,
lava lips blew
smoke rings at god and
you became alone.
You have hidden
in black branches, upside-
down, hunted at night,
muscles tense and sliding
hide, gliding like cloud,
black ink, as your markings
themselves glide, flow, blotch,
rosette, roll, a shoal of
shadow on sand, rain runs
slantways as you hunt,
pooling, prowling,
fern fronds part for you.
You are the littlest big one,
the littlest ancient,
marginalia to the ravelling
spool of forest's page,
through mangrove and menggaris,
it is all ablaze;
spotfires in your eyes.
You do not strike fear
but you are often afraid —

your life is all yearning, slurring,
chuffing to low moan,
hissing, shitting
macaque bones on the
numberless paths,
and within
your trembling soul,
the hunger, always
the hunger.

But it is true —
you are free, sometimes,
when the fires sleep and
the moon is just so,
to be leopard,

to dance on treetops.

I FELL ASLEEP DYING OF THIRST BUT WHEN I WOKE UP I SWEAR I HEARD A WATERFALL

MAHAKAM RIVER

The cadavers of giants are being lugged past —
legless, armless, decapitated — and on other barges,
piled up in pyramids, hard brown livers and burning
hearts in pieces, coughed up through chutes from the
killing field and haloed by their own dust — I lie on
the deck and watch them go by. Me, driven wild or
lethargic by longing, minute, minute, hour, diesel ghosts
and nasi kuning, fried fish heavy with heavy metals —
up from Samarinda, I am sailing, this journey so many
have made, brown highway connecting the tribes of the
interior to the Makassar Strait. At river's mouth crumble
stone teeth, traces of Kutai Martadipura, the oldest civilisation
in Indonesia, where the ojek boys rest on their bikes and fish
and flirt; I watch the swiftlets whir and flit, harden spit
for bird's nest soup, on a reverse *Heart of Darkness*.
Instead of a foolhardy European travelling into the centre,
fearing headhunters and cannibals, I am journeying to
the interior of me. Local myths say you go upriver to the
land of the dead, but right now, it feels like life reborn. Softly
I hover the eddies — dark silt bed might make good grave.
Wayfarer in the homeland — I could never think of Ireland
that way, though that is the other half. The locals think I am
Arab until they hear me speak Bahasa, poorly, and ask for
pictures of my family — ya, kamu orang Dayak — then sell
me embroideries and tell me it is election season. They say
the capital of Indonesia is soon going to be moved here.
Jakarta is sinking into the sea.

I reach a point where I can go no further,
but not the source — never, it seems, the source.

Mr Muhammad holds up the skull of a leopard; he shot it
in the jungle. There are human skulls in the roof of the
longhouse — 'we don't take heads anymore. Well, it's okay
if someone's *really* bad' — stories carved in the
beams, boars and buttocks, things I will never understand.
The men are re-skinning a drum, smoking, wrapping
it tightly into place with sinew, testing it for resonance,
calling in a storm that beats its own rhythm, on the streets and
river, falling syllables, like 99 names of God, repeated,
and all the spirit names of animal and ancestor.

My skin, silver with rain — touch it with the tuning fork.
      I promise, it echoes too.

NUTMEG

Cobalt divined from beneath those waves, the same colour, foamy, horse-headed, surging at the side of the boat, white mane shredding away in steady beats of bubble and spray, the tiny ripples beyond a topography, shuddering ridges and valleys, deep blue-black on the swell and silver at the fringes, sun high up and the ocean singing light back to itself, run hands at the side of the boat and it is warm as amniotic fluid or arak held in the mouth.

Look! That's Pulau Run. To control the world's nutmeg trade, the Dutch bartered Manhattan to the English for that little island.

The couple didn't stop to see it, this forgotten El Dorado, just a kilometre long and lost in blue embrace. They continued on to another island. When they arrived, they booked a cooking course and a boat tour, then settled into the converted colonial manor and, fuelled by nutmeg soup and fresh tuna fishballs, candlenut-lathered eggplant and cake, made love with the vehemence of those who know the final port is just beyond the horizon. They stood on the grand balcony and smoked kretek, felt the cool tiles on their feet, took selfies with the rosé dusk and dead volcano behind them — a little world, a world of their projection, just for a moment. Shadow puppets acting out an epic. Behind them, below, were the ruins of a Dutch fort — buried by a thousand greens — and kids playing football. They later found out a massacre had once occurred there, the attempted extermination of a race, all for spice.

Butter and flour the pan, sayang. Beat in the sugar and butter, fold in the egg. Set it in stages — test it for *doneness*. The layers will not appear until it is sliced — there are many, so many it hurts. Sprinkle on top, as a garnish, for taste,

a little nutmeg.

TWO WEEKS
THEIR WORLD A HOTEL ROOM
SHE SMELLED LIKE
NUTMEG AND BREWING MONSOONS

GHOST FOREST

WRITTEN IN COLLABORATION WITH TISHANI DOSHI

A forest flooded by a plastic sea. Tree trunks and
roots are all underwater — only branches pierce the
molten surface, jinned, white as vapour, jinns slowly
upwelling, silver leaves engraved by a razor. Song —
there is yet song throughout this city of ghost trees.
Two singers, cloaked in leopard skin, horned with antler,
pole a boat slowly over these plastic ripples, trying to
convince each other they're not alone. One hears
footsteps above. The other is certain a travelling
show follows at a distance, wordless troubadours who
magic the wood and eat twilight. Below: the world where
they once played, loved, filled their mouths with tapai and
chilli crab and wild ginger, ingested history, chewed future
without knowing. Swallowed a forest whole. They are
like statues, broken and marbled, wraithed in smoke.

The last woman and man in the world tie their boat to an
eave of the building where they once prayed, and harmonise.

Everything they touch is there because they speak its name.

CHILL THE FK OUT

BABY FOREST

(TANA TORAJA)

In that forest, babies who died before they had teeth
were placed into carved nooks in upright breadfruit
trees, bound into place with pandanus leaf or some
such, and after a while, the tree closed over and
folded soft bones into hardwood, and all that
remained was a ghostly outline, a thin scar like
an alcove or a door with no keyhole.

He saw her, his tall tree — his rainbow eucalyptus —
way down the years, crossing the road, with a baby
on her back, hugging onto those swimmer's shoulders,
the spangled skin he'd kissed so many times,

the child's smile so bright it drowned him in ivory.

MAKASSAR

FOR ABDI AND LILY

"God has made the earth and the sea,
and has divided the earth among men
and made the sea common to all"

— Sultan of Makassar to the Dutch ambassador, 1650

Squids in pools of ink; every vision of fish — moon-coloured,
see-through, hi-viz yellow, butterfly-pea blue, gold; some are the
size of a playing card, some bayonets; barracuda, wide-eyed tuna,
surprised, with the gasp going outta them; striped prawns & bound
crabs; fat clams exactly the size of a rich man's dinner plate. The men
who fish the fish, who ply them, carry brimming baskets, slung on a
bending pole, or two-handed, with nimble, stuttering step, dodging the
crowd with practised precision, sneakers scrawled with viscera and blood.
Hoodies, helmets, bandanas about the neck. Steam. Swearing. Prayer.
Kretek smoke ribbons through rows of mopeds. Smartphones and fish
scales, sop konro and coto Makassar. Rows of boom-boom rooms, a
twelve-year-old being smoked by a cigarette. The rise of the hardline
binds centuries of cross-pollination in this hive, mercantile drive still
gallops over reclaimed land. Zig-zag lontara on palm-leaf manuscript, fading.
Genealogies, maps, creation myths, each 'four-cornered' letter standing
for the elements that created the cosmos — fire, air, earth, water —

      the rain

      the rain

      the rain

I was once told that all things have a navel, a central passageway
for the soul — person, village, cosmos. Even ships have a navel
drilled into the keel before they are allowed to set sail.
Loyalty might compel me to say that Borneo is the navel of Nusantara,
but in truth, it is on the island shaped like an orchid. It is Makassar.
This is the place the perahus left, sailed for a land they called Marege —
Yolngu Country, Arnhem Land — to exchange words and smoke,
purple-inked bêche-de-mer. Red flag dance, tamarind trees, smokehuts
remain, an alternate history to the white sails of British hawkishness.
Rock paintings on either end of the trade route. I took a boat, a motorbike,
then walked through jungle, got so close I could smell the sap that bound
the ancient pigment — revenant men fighting on horseback, boiling suns,
and again and again, humans upright in boats, peering towards

      the waves

      the waves

      the waves

Throughout these seas, all seas, claims are pinned on the fluid;
tattoos on liquid face — no border lines can ever hold.
Why? is a weight that drops into fathomless dark and all that
remains is a shudder on the surface of the deep. The border
disperses before the hand that signed it into law can finish
writing the first letter of its name. The border will be
scooped up, laved, shat into, drunk, spat out in Peru,
used to distil whiskey in Ireland, and may, one day, come back
into my hands in Makassar, where I pour it over my face. When
that day comes, and border returns to the latitude where
someone tried to name it, its name is now changed, dancing on a

      braid of kelp, spoken in sand.

FAKE ISLANDS

there are fake islands in the South China Sea /
military bases on reclaimed ground / a runway on an atoll /
a propeller jewelled in salt / a whim of lava /
ringed by tides' disquiet /

migratory birds /
bear witness to the weft and warp of borders /
the loom of nations / the pedal turns the wheel /
the truant threads / if any / are fraying /
an inconsistent tapestry /

from the deep / fish look upwards /
see the blurred crucifix of a bird / or fighter jet /

a shaking lens /
      the ocean

Sometimes I feel like an atoll.

Structures are built on me I did not consent to.

But perhaps, at times, I invited them,
        and of course, I do the same,
            floating on my little raft, looking for land.

That which you choose to portray —
inviting fire-tips of coral, the crescent of sand
so alluring for beach-seeking bottle —
            is never what it seems.

Words can be fake islands, people too.

I should have been a dancer.

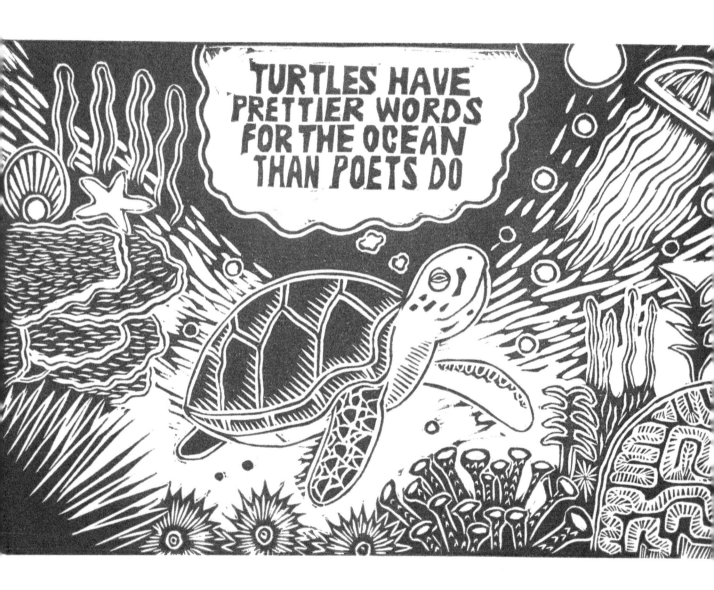

INGAT

You, the bad boy of Malaysian poetry,
asleep on my parents' floor, muttered
and rolled under sarong's sensuous
canopy, shuddered electro aftershocks,
but a waking smile so wide, wider
even than the heart is wide, swore with joy
and recited Romantic poetry, declared
you exclusively ate bananas — then you
marked a Malay proverb in a book,
and gifted it to me with a scribbled note:

Ingat juga akar kau dua —
anggapkau hakikat in satu
anugerah yang mahakuasa.

'Remember also the two roots of your heritage —
treat this fact as a gift full of divine power.'

I was seventeen, Sisqó-haired
with spot pimples and jerry-rigged bravado.

You must have forseen what I'd face
in the great southern robber state. You,
in all black with a red bandana,
once kicked out of a pub for being
unAustralian. Or back in Malaysia,
pissing on the pamphlets of the self-satisfied —
poetic apostate, unlikely Malay, dervish
mind whirling to get closer to a profane god.

Salleh, I carried your words like an amulet,
though a divine power bedevilled me
most nights — janitor of no-man's-land,
sweeping up zeroes, bottle in hand — ya,
you knew those devils too, they were legion,
         in bottle and buzz-saw brain.

I could never write a pantun with ease,
never learned properly the tongue of my blood,
but did write, like you, letter upon single letter —
those letters made words, those words made poems,
and sometimes they looked like a procession of angels,
         dressed in black.

I tried to find you some years back, to thank you
for the amulet, sacred and profane,
but not *that* hard. The trail went dead —
I looked up from the page and the moment had fled.

We write, we die,
we pass softly through each other's lives,
flying through night like a magical keris,

         or diamond bright stream

         of a galactic chain of piss.

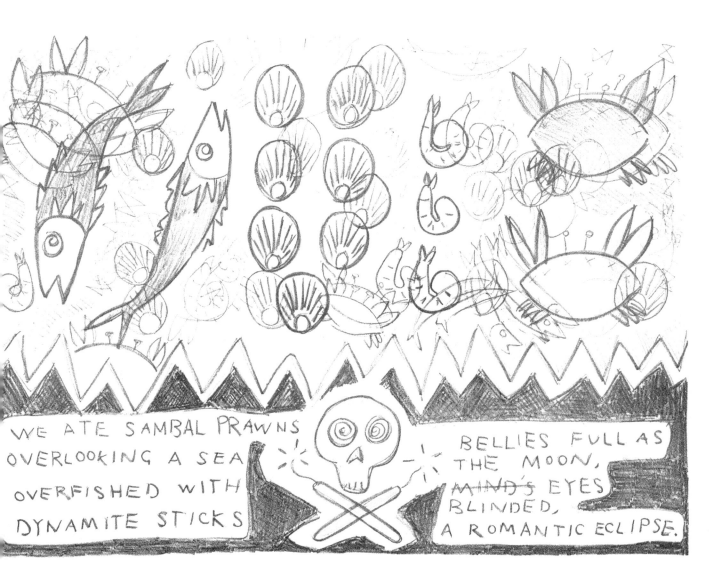

WE ATE SAMBAL PRAWNS
OVERLOOKING A SEA
OVERFISHED WITH
DYNAMITE STICKS

BELLIES FULL AS
THE MOON,
MIND'S EYES
BLINDED,
A ROMANTIC ECLIPSE.

HUNGRY
GODS

Let me loose on that broth, Auntie — how much? Bah. Ladled with
intent, the whole archipelago is here in this roiling coconut cream, stirred

by a literal marriage. China, India, Champa, Siam, Penang, Borneo —
such happy sailing into the vortex. Can you smell that? Sedaaaaap!

Vermicelli the long-threaded trade route backwards in time — tamarind,
ketumbar, kalamansi lime, prawn heads dancing on lemongrass mat.

The sea is two blocks away. Stateless people — thousands of them.
Hauling in prawns — millions of them. My tongue burns at the thought.

Makan! We are all complicit. Sneers at mentions of exotic food
in ethnic lit all boil up into the steam that snakes to heaven, bristling

the nose hairs of hungry gods, patron saints of food and yearning, eyes
crossed with enlightenment, tastebuds puddling for one more chilli hit of truth.

The knowing is in the eating.

Slurp.

LIFE

LOVE

LAKSA

OBM

TIKAR

FOR YEE I-LANN

sit your bum down on this woven mat   the geography of the house

a map   laid flat   pandanus fibres crisscrossed   dream atop

it pray atop it   dry chilli, fish, nutmeg   yarn atop it   the

dripping weight of yarn atop it   dye, ink, mordent   use it to wrap

the dead   like a page   flat, two-dimensional, but   the functions

are vertical   no need for art to be autocratic, as I once thought   all

equal, let us create, cross-pollinate   sit around this tikar with me a while

Me and my uncle Bakri

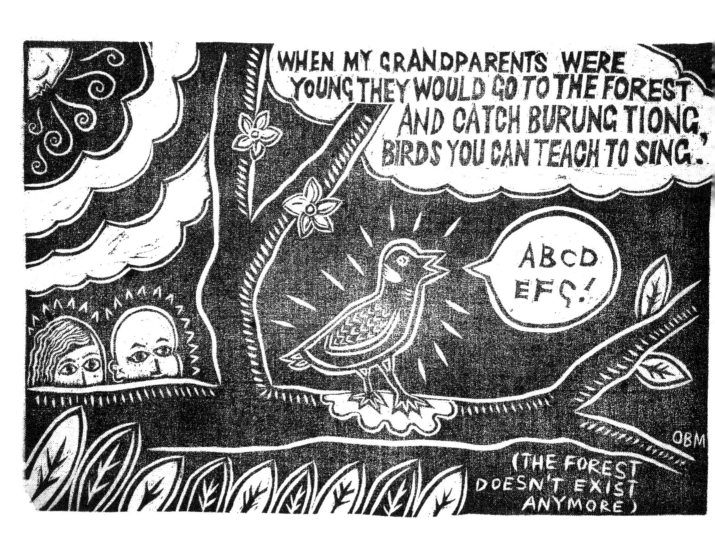

MILE 7, SANDAKAN

A later me wouldn't have done it —
split the turtle egg open, splash it with kecap manis,
slurp it down raw, oily yolk and thick white,
then reach into the purple plastic ice-cream
container for another. Makan — she said, it's a treat,
when I lived on the street these were like gold.
We ate roast pigeon too, that night,
crunching bite-sized wings not five-hundred metres
from where the Death Camp had been.
A later me swims with the turtles
and thinks them divinity incarnate, despairs
how hunger makes men raid nests
and barter shell for cigarettes and diesel.

Thoughts you have underwater:

there's always a reason for the way a person is;
turtles they move, they move like birds —
they scull, they glide, they wing;
oh, how much freight can a soul bear?
More than a poem, surely. Not nearly as much.
Is a foul mouth hereditary, from
matriarch to grandson? Who the fuck knows.
My mind — it chews thoughts like jellyfish.
Does telling your grandmother's story
count as appropriation? No. Yes. Surely.
A fish-bomb, heard underwater,
is a dull concussion like the banging of a gong,
a car crash in space.

A later me idolises my grandmother,
writes her into poems as a paragon of survival
and resilience. A later me still sees
her petty prejudices,
her fire-starting, batu api heart.

There's always a reason. Always.

In Mile 7, the swinging bulb,
the ice-cream container, the pigeon bones,
the geckoes saying *cikcak*, *cikcak*.
Her hands were
leathery as turtle-egg shells,
squeezing mine, squinting —
makan, Omar, these will
make you clever at having babies
and help you see in the dark.

AN ORANGUTAN USED TO WATCH MY DAD READ QURAN EACH MORN
وَمَا مِن دَابَّةٍ
BUT EVEN SCRIPTURE COULDN'T SAVE HIM WHEN THE LOGGERS CAME
OBM
"DO NOT FORGET US" HE WHISPERS

WHEN FACED WITH UNCONQUERABLE ODDS—
FUEDAL LORDS OR VIOLENT COLONIAL MASTERS,
THE VILLAGERS TURNED TO ALLEGORIES
TO SUBVERT THE POWER OF THE RICH,
ESPECIALLY THE TALE OF SANG KANCIL,

THE WILY MOUSEDEER, WHO, DESPITE
HIS PHYSICAL FRAILTY, USES HIS
SMARTS TO OUTWIT MUCH BIGGER FOES
LIKE SI BELANG, THE TIGER

WERETIGER

The tiger trapper said:

A man-eating tiger always attacks
from behind, never front-on, because
when every person in this world is born,
an inscription from the Qur'an is etched
into their forehead, proclaiming man's
superiority over all living things.

This, the tiger cannot stand.

*

Once, all across the archipelago,
tiger fights were staged by rulers for their subjects.
They were pitted against creatures that
were seen as peaceful, like elephants or buffaloes,
representing the stability of the state. The tigers'
mouths would be sewn shut; they would
be tethered to a stake. The fights were rigged
so that the tiger, a symbol of disorder and wildness
— the enemy of the state — would lose.

*

Too good to be true — I should have known it was,
when I raced like a low rolling fire through the undergrowth
towards the bleating goat, propelled by a circular cadence
in sinew and blood, carrying me towards the rightful end —
my teeth crunching down to un-piece neck bones and squeeze
from the goat its life force. Oh, such sweet joy, but only for a
second, before the collapse, the cunning cage — the trap that
shatters me to gold dust.

My cellmates are two clouded leopards and a panther.

No more the forest, no more the cane that reflected my burning bright.
Human shapes are cheering in the distance. Within the royal
courtyard, my flattened ears can hear them shaking the world.

Even as they cheer, their voices tremble.

Yes, I have been primed to lose,

    yet they still fear me.

BENDERA BORNEO

VEXILLOLOGY *the study of flags.*

VEXILLOGRAPHY *the art and practice of designing flags.*

The flag of North Borneo (1882–1942) has a Union Jack in the canton and, opposite, a British lion within a yellow, sun-like circle. Like many predatory beasts of heraldry, the lion in chief is rampant — paws raised, it pounces, it roars. North Borneo was controlled, at first, not by Britain itself but by a British trade company, determined to acquire and exploit resources. In an unknown year, my grandmother was born beneath this flag. Despite illiteracy, selling cigarettes and tapping rubber, she devised fifty rhyming poems in her head, which she still knows today. On Labuan, an island off the coast, she birthed her first child at thirteen or fourteen, to a Scottish seaman, who left soon after. The child was taken by the state.

From 1942 to 1945, the flag bore a different sun — the rising sun of the Imperial Japanese Army. My step-grandfather can still recite the Japanese anthem, which he learnt as a child. Every time he does it, he mimes raising that flag. This practice was beaten into him in Sandakan, where the Japanese infamously marched thousands of Australians to death. These same Allied/Anzac forces also bombed several towns to bits, killing thousands of locals. My grandfather's hands became calloused from the rope that raised the Japanese flag.

From 1945 to 1963, the flag of the Crown Colony of North Borneo replaced the yellow circle with a white one, inside of which a brown hand and a white hand grip a flag that bears the same British lion as before, but much smaller now. The brown and white hands represent the unity of the native and European populations, though you may notice that the white hand grips the flagpole a little higher up. My father was born beneath this flag, in a logging camp in Sandakan.

In 1963, Malaysian Borneo was divided into two territories, Sabah and Sarawak, which had an agreement with Peninsula Malaya that they would be equal partners in the modern state of Malaysia. There had been several options for Sabah and Sarawak, including autonomy, joining Indonesia or joining the Philippines. In 1976, Sabah and Sarawak became mere states in a federation within Malaysia. Some say a new form of colonisation began. The Sabah flag's design includes a stripe of yellow (gold), to represent the state's riches. In the top left-hand corner is a green canton, to represent the abundant forests, against which is the silhouette of the sacred Mount Kinabalu, in the same brown as the arm that gripped the flag within a flag.

The Sabah flag from 1982 to 1988 looks (to me) quite similar to that of the Philippines. I was born during this time, on a red island very different from Borneo, but my bloodline runs on both sides of the contested border between Malaysia and the Philippines. I have read that some Kadazan-Dusun peoples were enraged that Mount Kinabalu was left off this flag. Upon returning to Sabah for the first time since childhood, I climbed Mount Kinabalu and saw from its peak a restless ocean of clouds. I couldn't walk for days afterwards. My grandfather massaged my calves with his still-calloused hands. 'Senyum adalah sedakah,' he said. A smile is charity.

The current Sabah flag was introduced in 1988, and is an update of the 1963 version. The forest green has disappeared now, as has the gold of state riches. The overwhelming colour is blue — zircon blue for *peace and calmness*, icicle blue for *unity and prosperity*, and Mount Kinabalu in royal blue for *peace and harmony*. In the past, these blues were not soothing to me; they looked like an upset, like tormented waves of a contested sea. But nowadays, I don't mind the way they ripple multi-tinted, I see more clearly the balancing chunk of red — like chilli, like bloodline. Still, I wonder what right I have to comment.

In early 2020, I visited Semporna, on the east coast. The Philippines is a stone's throw away, and many stateless people — not Malaysian, not Filipino — live there in abject poverty, without medical care, without rights. Luminous coral reefs have been fish-bombed to pieces. People in the streets were just beginning to wear masks, fearful of coronavirus.

I set out for the first time on the Sulu Sea, a place where my biological grandfather's people, the Suluk or Tausug ('Men of the Currents'), have sailed for centuries. I would like to say it felt like homecoming, but it felt more like tourism. As I left the shore, I saw a traditional lepa lepa houseboat of the Bajau-Sama Laut, sometimes called 'Sea Gypsies' or 'Pala'u', with flags whipping from its masts — vibrant, celebratory, a ragged chain of rainbow fire.

I am a man with no flag, unless you count the page in front of me. Maybe that is my white flag. I surrender to it daily, I deface it, I daub it with my myths; never the right arrangement to truthfully tell the stories within my borders; always false, always reductive. Yet as the light dies and yearns, I let it flutter, because I must. It is all I have.

Here is land, I say. *This is land.*

I AM A HOMELAND

TANAH
— earth.

AIR
— water (sea).

TANAH AIR
— homeland.

Aku tanah air.

I am a homeland

weighted to the ocean floor by a moral conundrum.
On the waking edge between forested life and
limitless sleep, sand is scalloped like an ear —
it hears, listens, fizzes, rustles. Hold breath like
confession, sayang, now let go in rhythm.

Inhale   —   I am singular.
Exhale   —   I appear in many places.

South, south-west, the pirate winds go through my slatted
bones, bind me in smoke, romanticism fattens and bloats
around the liver, realpolitik an electroshock to the heart,
coins sink upwards out of my pores and stories are engraved
with my blood; durian husks and potato skins on these shores

Inhale   —   I am yearning.
Exhale   —   I am inconsequence.

I hear them call me an illegitimate kingdom — fake Muslim,
snake-oil trade port, banana republic, middle-class mirage.
An empty plot where the rivers commingle. Orchids and torch
ginger, my garlands have started to rot, the plastic fish mounte
on the wall is singing its last poorly penned jingle.

Inhale   —   I am fraud.
Exhale   —   I am truth.

North, north-east. I am a land of disorder. My
existence — resistance— to admin and trade companies,
cannons and capital. Colonisers fuck me with mechanical
dicks to extract my hidden glint. Drill down into my flesh
and there lie the oil wells that will set the forest aflame.

Inhale   —   I am anger.
Exhale   —   I am acceptance.

At times I am glacial peak and polar ice caps, but hard shards,
sharp from chiselling, melt and become the rising tide, the eagle's
swoop swells to tempest, typhoon, cyclonic midnight marauder.
There never has been, never will be a force of nature like me, the
monsoonal flow state over the loose leaf. Bruce Lee
Inhale   —   I am cliché.
Exhale   —   I am ambiguity

impossible to bear it seems, these days. The
words tanah and air are combined in me, ocean and
earth, land people, sea people, once warring factions,
but two parts combined into a necessary whole.
The tide reverses, often. I am no one   thing.

Inhale

Exhale

IMPOSSIBILITY (draft seven)

I get an email from a friend, from ███████████
███████████, a poet who'd started his own movement.
A poetry movement with one member.

    Nice to hear from you,my bro. ...
    Future here is very dark. ..uncertain. .
    No words to express. .
    All alphabets are eliminated. ███████████
    But resiliance is impossibility of poetry of human condition. ..
    every moment is beyond words. ..

███████████confounding, esoteric, a jumble
of abstract images and non-sequiturs. Words███████
ghosts. ███████████abstraction███████████
purpose, ███████████
███████████ threat █████, coding ███████
███████essential. No one can ███████████say,
'Aha! These words defy███████'

But if they want to come for you, they will█████

█████Shostakovich —███████████shaping notes
███████████ 'camouflage'.

█████stone to sinking stone ███████████ *How does power refract?*
There are many fiefdoms in the kingdom

The stakes are not so high in Australia. But figuratively — relatively — does the killshot crack from an enemy turret or come point-blank ██████████████████████████████████████? Where and why do I pause the pen, lift its tread from the racetrack?

I am finding it impossible to express what I mean.

All ███████████ are eliminated . . .

There was a book burning in Borneo, ████████. *Allegedly.* A mass grave of books — records of Indigenous language and culture. Forests set on fire. Not by the British, but by ████████ ███████████ *Allegedly.* Even if this event did not occur, the 'discouragement' of Indigenous language songs and TV shows, the banning of teaching those languages in school, ████████████████

████████████████

██████████████████████████████████████

██████████████████████████ a forest into oil palm.

Bonsai a mind long enough and, after a while, it prunes itself.

Sometimes the only book that remains # is the age-old playbook of power

MAZES

FOR LUNA VIDYA

'There is a village in Jeneponto
whose name I forget — they butcher horses
there for food. On the beach on the headland, there
is a cemetery, and in it, a big, old tamarind tree. By night,
it is covered by so many fireflies it becomes as
bright as a lighthouse, and fishermen use it
to guide themselves back to shore.
They say that fireflies are a dead
person's spirit, you know?
A special type of light.
A light to lead
you home.'

I'm probably remembering her story wrong.

'I was once on a boat with a blind shaman.
He did nothing for days but water the decks —
they were constantly wet. There came a day when
we were stuck on a reef and couldn't find a way out.
The crew was going mad. Mansur challenged Arif to
a dagger duel — both were to be encircled by a sarong
so neither could back down. The blind shaman sprang up,
stood at the prow for a long time. He was smelling the air.
He sniffed,   this way and that,   carefully.   Then he pointed.
Wherever the shaman pointed, the captain steered the boat,
and soon, like magic, we were out of the razorblade maze
and out on open water. "You see, the air above the
reef smells heavy," said the shaman, "but the air
above clear water smells *thin* and *clean*.
That is how I knew which way to go."'

I wondered: is it possible to smell your
way out of a forest on fire?

FATBERGS AND FIRENADOES/SILKEN FACED
DEVILS WITH BARBED WIRE HALOES/MANKIND
MINED FOR WATER ON A BURNING MOONSCAPE/
I LAPPED A LAKSA, DREAMING OF MY MAGIC PLACE.

RAINBOW ROADKILL

An archipelago   on

a river of tar, silent they

resolve into death-shape as

he approaches. He has

weaved through many such islands

in this Country aflame, humpbacked,

       rounded forms, fraying, split into

separatist parts, national

emblems turned carrion — kangaroo,

wombat, echidna, emu, koala — or

introduced fauna — fox, rabbit, deer,

tyre snake, leather shoe —

so many final attitudes, wistful or

appalled, grinning or grim, sorry jesters

and restive priests, some

are marked with neon Xs, yellow

and pink, *this one has been checked for*

signs of life, it says, do not bother here,

drive on.

But a particular

islet, very

tiny,

snares his

attention: a rainbow lorikeet,

feathered phantasmagoria of

green, yellow, mauve.

There is something

more unjust about a bird

roadkilled — *aren't they*

supposed to be, quite

literally, above all

this?

In the suck of air

as he zooms past,

the lorikeet's body stays

perfectly still,

but a single wing lifts,

like a migrant at a port.

Two days prior,

the man had sat on a

balcony, flipping the same

coin for three hours straight.

From the gum trees, spectral,

a rainbow lorikeet had

sailed down in a sudden,

kaleidoscopic trill.

The bird jinked and

bobbed along the rail, chewed

seed and tilted its

head, curious

and unafraid — it made him

smile to see it, the deep

blue belly and head, the

yellow chest, the

thighs green as a reviving fern.

X.

It carried the coin away.

PRECIOUS
THING,
VANISHING
THING

Life and Death on the Queanbeyan River

SONG OF THE FROG

ha ha — you could say i earned these stripes — black on
        yellow,
each one unique as the fingerprints of the men whose
        hands gripped
musket and spade, each stripe unique as the snowflakes
        that fall soft
around us final few — ha haaaa — i creak my gallows
        laughter out into
the long, snowy dark, out, over the creeks and granite
        tors, the florets of
moss like slow stellar explosions, my song scrapes along
        the valleys and
rock floors searching for purchase, nocturne for my
        ravaged clutch and
rangy beloved — the stripes on his belly were cornflower
        blue, we fed
each other upland psalms and buried our eyes in the stars
        above the land.

first it was brumbies, then it was the pigs.

even before the men, into our world rampaged those
           bundles of muscle and tusk,
hoof, hot breath and nostril, slicing up turf and tussock,
           shitting on our heads,
chewing up our sphagnum to shit on us again,
           forewarning of the pale men whose
frostbitten words slalom down the icy crevasses and
           fallen snow gums — they
redirect history and dam a world, the turbines turn and
           warm their homes, our homes
interned, warmed, in turn, like turning globe, burning,
           heating up like fresh powder on
a dinnerplate in a microwave, crushed up by credit card in
           alpine lodge, it is snow season
in more ways than one — haa haaaa, i'm the funny one
           again — if you can't laugh, you die —

before they had their pandemic, we had ours — were are
           losing our minds — our skin crawls with devils — no-
           one can say from whence it came, we spread madness
           to each other — there is another world where this
           never happened — but in this world, we are held in
           shipping containers — all straight lines — our only
           hope — by creatures with test tubes and microscopes and

underfunded visions — we have more in common with
them than might first appear — they, like us, are not
believed — like us, a dying breed.

you can hold me in your palm — dazed — i can hold
you in my eye — blink once if you're being held
against your will, you say — in one blink — *blink* — a
millennium becomes a matter of days —

UNAUSTRALIA

Lemme tell you what's unAustralian, mate.

  Australia.

It's time we shuffle
this country off to Deed Poll
  I reckon,
sign the papers,
add two letters
&
rename it *UnAustralia*.

UnAustralia!

An ill-advised artwork
defined by negative space,
we define selves by what they are not;
  crude white lies told in blackface.

Come watch the parade!

  in UnAustralia

  Land of the fair-skinned,
   Fairy Bread,
   Fair Go.

Let's put a shark net around the island,
      & mummify childhoods in barbed-wire
      but please,
      make sure it's 5000 kays
          outta sight, outta mind,
      so we can relish
            our snap-crackle-*pop-pop-pop-pop-POP!*

Watch Froot Loops bounce around the porcelain,
      same colour as a flag
      we wipe our arses on
      when we take a PlebiShite…

Go postal

      in UnAustralia

      Land of the Culture Wars —
      get crop-dusted
      by heroin white noise of bureaucracy,
      stunned & softened up,
      now jingo grenades
      bomb sense of self
          to phantom limb.

AXE THE TAX
STOP THE BOATS
AUSSIE AUSSIE AUSSIE!

Oi,
it's UnAustralia!

where politicians roll up shirtsleeves,
& go panning in the Main Stream
          (the River Formerly Known as Shit Creek),
sift up nuggets of Fool's Gold,
but not even a mining boom
          could buy compassion…
they smear Vegemite vows on the toilet wall…

          That which was written, that which was hidden,
          punch-drunk love left the barflies smitten,
          Drive It Like You Stole It, get in where you fit in,
          the brakes wear out when a nation's joy-ridden.

It's UnAustralia…

          hear voices detonate
          from tuckshop to quarter-acre block:

FREEDOM OF SPEECH! FREEDOM OF SPEECH!

But beware the fine print, my friends

          all need not apply

If you're Black/brown/Muslim/woman/queer/smart/loud/
          and you dare question a cross-eyed sacred cow,

they'll twine newspaper headlines
to a noose & lynch you
          from a Daily Telegraph poll

          in UnAustralia —

LIFE IS
A COMEDY SHOW
PUT ON BY
A FUNERAL HOME,
A DARK JOKE
FROM AN
ANGEL'S LIPS
ON A
PRISON
TELEPHONE

HELLO, BROTHER

dedicated to Haji-Daoud Nabi and the
victims and survivors of the Christchurch Massacre

my marrow is a sponge steeped in rum,
my septum and heart are covered in crystals,
rashes of them, shimmering scabs of them —
with each pulse, they burst forth a new tumour made of quartz.

i draw my sleeves down to cover my tattoos...

standing there, on the pavement,

there, where it is too much to bear, there
are roses and letters, pounamu greenstone
and candles burned way down, and a banner
of hope stretched as taut as a nerve:

ALLAH BLESS OUR COUNTRY, LAND OF LOVE AND COMPASSION.

kids are playing on the steps while their parents
make ablutions, ready, still, for prayer. 'make sure
the water goes above the ankle and the elbow!' i hear my father say.

i cannot enter, though i have no doubt i would be welcome.

Hello, Brother.

the man's last words before armageddon.

rice   tea   hands   smiles   cloth   whispers   shrouds

despite everything that is, and everything that isn't,

these people and i share something
not spelled out in any book (perhaps),
or even in falling rain
or smoke rising from the mouth of a gun.

still, i cannot enter.

but i raise my hands, cupped lightly to say Duha.

Inna Lillahi wa inna ilayhi wa raji'un.

when i was a kid,
i used to imagine that if i held my hands this way,
tipped slightly forward, i could catch rain,
and if i held perfectly still, the glassy water
in my palms would become a mirror,
or better yet, a *window*,
through which i might be able to see God.

i never did.

today, my hands catch tears
and although the water sways and shivers,
for just a moment, i think, it stands

      still.

SAID SCENT

they breathed each other in / the oxygen signatures of skin / and language broke down then /

I don't know

Idontknow

idontknow

idonoidonoidono

but their skin knew / spoke / a secret script / spoke sun-gilt flank and tear-damp hair / crumbed washing powder and coffee half-drunk / lemongrass lotion and b.o. / spoke a filet-o-fish and a craig david playlist / spoke sesame seeds ground in ripple-combed mortar / dumplings hand-folded and steamed in bamboo / wood ear mushroom steeped in soy, chianking vinegar, ginger, garlic, chilli / spoke a long, long walk by the ancient river / where snakes double-helix in new skins / bright birds scull against mongrel hour / clouds grapefruit pink / spoke a cherry tree's weeping habit / a petal each for the times they'd run it back / spoke homegoing and thunderclap / the wet wool of a red flag / *several* / a coffin sewn with poems / and the hardly worn brass of a spare key, handed back /

cousin of taste / molecules heavy with memory / scatter / a quickening fire / shatter / pollen's glittering glide / we laughed lots and laughed with ease / said scent / in a storm of hair, smiling into each other's vows / float like a leaf from a brittle gum / shine like a buried gun / *never*, said scent, said scent *we know now* / it echoes like sound / infinite divisions down to the zero / the willing, the un-willing / mango skins, binned / sticky sweet bleed of a mercy killing / said scent i'll miss you but i do not love you / the same / said i love you forever and i am the one to blame /

they never saw each other again / the only true word that would remain / the murmur of scent

LEOPARD BEACH

Rowing through smoke, rolling black roses,
scudding over spirits on fire.
My shoulders scream their hinges weak,
each opaline blister hisses and sweats.
Cheek to deck, boat bucks, drool drips.
I know that I am dying. I want to know.

I raise a shaky fingertip and carve the smoke
into the shape of a headland.
Upon it, I draw a green drapery, and a tamarind tree,
and by jabbing my finger, embroider it with fireflies.
Last of all, I trace out a soft white scimitar of sand.
I have made land.
Hit shore, weep in the shallows,
tear my clothes to make a flag.

I name this place Leopard Beach.

100% body positive, 100% plastic free!
The sky — you can see the sky here! Look how blue it is!
The arts are valued and funded. Men do not beat their wives —
there are no men, there are no wives.
And you are here, and you! ... and you.
There is such a thing as forgiveness. And quiet.

Hate mail burns up before it reaches shore,
but the homeless and refugees are given safe
passage here. Salve for their smoking shoulders,
we search the sky for shooting stars…

Ah! Even in my Shangri-la,
there are the homeless and refugees —
my dreams not pure enough
to clarify a world where nothing is wrong.

'Man child,' I hear a voice say. 'Leopard boy:
a utopia is a dangerous place.
The longer you stay, the harder life upon return.'

It might be me.

No. Indulge me a moment this naivety —
I am tired and ageing and home is on fire.
A dreamland might inspire a could-be world.

By day, I slake my thirst and clean my fur
'til the clouds shine obsidian.

By night, I look towards the fire that is home,
and imagine it is a bright aurora on a holy meridian.

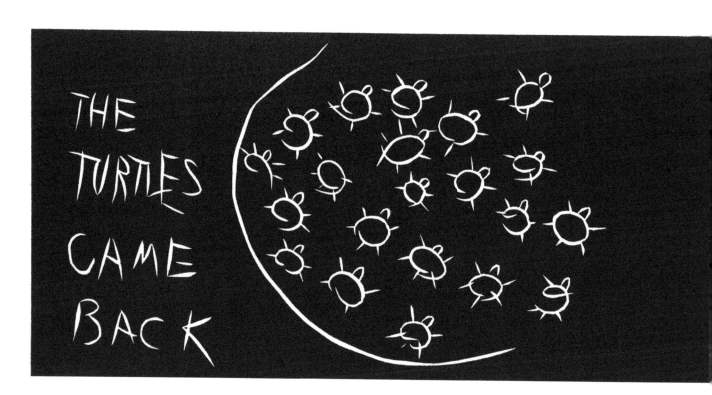

We cleaned up the beach

(Tale)

AFLOAT ON THE BLAZING MIRROR OF SEA,
WE ONLY EVER FISH FOR WHAT WE NEED

WE WERE REBORN AS SALTWATER,
SUMMERTIME SPIRITS,
A SMOKE MADE CHOREOGRAPHY
OF FREESTYLED LYRICS.
WE OPENED UP A WORLD BEFORE UNIMAGINED,
SOON WE DRAPED KISSES
LIKE GARLANDS OF JASMINE

~~TAKE MY~~

~~KINDNESS FOR WEAKNESS~~

~~BE CRUEL~~
~~TO BE KIND~~

~~COS YOUR VISION~~
~~IS PERFECT~~

~~BUT MY LOVE~~
~~IS JUST BLIND~~

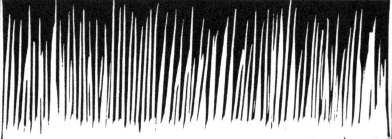

BIRDS OF THE MUSES
FOOTSOLDIERS OF A GODDESS
BORN FROM A TEAR
IN THE EYE OF THE SUN.
HUM HYMNS
IN THE FRAGILE CHAPEL,
SANCTIFY STARFALL,
SAVE US FROM OURSELVES &
BLESS OUR TONGUES WITH GOLD

Bees are Angels

CAPITAL

End to end, the hills —

Black Mountain, Mount Taylor, Mount Stromlo, Mount Majura, Mount Painter,
Mount Pleasant, Mount Ainslie, The Brindabellas.

Peaks renamed against sky's reach, amethyst smoke, two clouds — white and heavy as four
hundred drug busts, cranes with raptor machinations picking the bones, and everywhere,
trees —

brittle gum, kurrajong, alpine ash, manchurian pear, crepe myrtle, black cypress,
atlas cedar

sacred sites flooded for a lake, a concrete brink where people take their coffee and
walk retrievers; lolspeak, legalese, fuck-you-cunt and a thousand other forms of poetry;
hot chips and gravy, halal snack pack or quinoa, cold-dripped time, smoke in the chamber
and pill on the tongue.

at ground level, wild orchids, impossible to the untrained eye —

alpine swan, veined sun, pink spiral, spider, golden moth, purple beard

beyond what is seen or believed
        all   is hinterland.

breath explodes, white wattle,
        bartered for approaching night,

        the hills

        still here, still there.

RED

A Renaissance-style painting of a seated couple.

Neither is looking at the other, but their lips are slightly parted — the viewer might venture to think that words have just been spoken. Their skin has a certain flush, rendered carefully in umber, burnt sienna and ochre. Does it speak of excitement or dread?

Their eyes are cast downward, away from each other, and it is possible they reflect the hint of a carpark, or a man-made lake. They are sitting in a circular, concrete bus stop. A shivering shard of light in the man's iris, a single stroke of white paint, lends him an expression that says: you lie without knowing, you are not yet past the he who came before; how many times will we repeat this circular poem, this relentless heating and cooling of the blood? It's also possible that he is simply observing a shred of plastic tumbling past his feet. His lips are shaped as if blowing out smoke, or readying to say something else, a word that begins with 'W' — watch? when? wait? The woman's eyes are painted with a different resolve. They seem to say: this feels less duet and more call and response with yourself; the lines you write, so vehemently yearning, are flattering but *flattening* — I am no Muse, no Goddess. One hand is lightly touching his knee. A gesture of comfort, perhaps, or pushing him gently away into some borderland.

This is all speculation.

What is most striking about the painting is their clothes, and the way the artist has depicted them — hanging folds of vermillion, scarlet. It takes great skill and exactitude to create the impression of pleats and folds of cloth, light and shade a near hallucination. Their skin gives off a subtle brightness where their hands grip the fabric tightly.

They are cloaked in expectancy;   draped in red flags.

FLANNEL FLOWERS

Called forth from the scorched earth, flannel flowers bloom once
every fifty years, grey-pink umbrellas, tiny, feathered, furred like
moth wing, constellated across this burnt-out canyon; we trek through
blackened banksias, lignotubers twined and gnarled in the peat, their
burst pods like so many eyes and mouths, omnidirectional cameras,
pointed every which way: out, over the valley where the cliffs far beyond
are divided as if by design, upright planes down which pewter streams
when it rains, sometimes; up, at the bluest, memoryless sky; and towards
us, lunching in a hollow in the rock. Miri is crouching down with Kimi to
look at the flannel flowers in the dust, and the purple fringe lilies amongst
them, which are delicate beyond belief and last only for one day. Miri is
not to know that this might be the only time she (or we) will ever see these
blooms, inherit through touch their grace, touch them as if testing a new word —
Miri is two years old and her world yet ahead. The old couple who arrive as we
leave have come to sight them for the first and last time, like certain eclipses,
like comets, these heavenly bodies at our feet. Last week, Jesse saw a
woman shake ashes from the cliffs, out into the canyon where the winds
whistle and sing hymns beneath black cockatoos' wings, that riffle the
bracts and bow the heads of flannel flowers, who lay so long in refuge,
made possible by the perfect conspiracy of catastrophic fire, time — and deluge.

A FLAG

imagine a flag.

the flag is 2×4 metres,
        extra-reinforced for high winds,
        UV resistant with a double-stitched hem.

six white stars with razor-sharp edges,
        three heraldic crosses overlaid
            on ultramarine blue.

there is no flagpole,
        no concrete anchor,

               it ripples in the blackness of space,

                  slow and smooth wavelets,

                  like stingray wings in a remote reef.

now imagine from that darkness a hand,
        resolving in front of you —
            knuckles, tendons & lines of palmistry.

imagine the hand sculpts itself into a fist.

imagine this fist is wrapped around a lighter —

sky blue plastic &

pressurised gas.

thumb — spark — flint — *chka* — fire — soft — flame

brink of flame meets margin of cloth

the fabric of the flag
catches
ecstatically

it hisses, it pants, it yearns

at first we envision a conflagration
the size of our bleakest dreamings
some vivid hell
some old testament furnace
where heretics
are burned.

instead

the flag
melts immediately into a viscous ball
a searing hot

napalm blob

the size of a sheep's brain

it falls through space

gathering speed

momentum

the weight of what we are
         & what we will become

until we catch it in our mouths

like a dragon would

a cannonball it mistook for the

      sun

INDIGO

Uncut the silk, unblue the indigo, unwater the lilies, unmeet the you.

A moonflower, 25 grams worth, broken in half between
thumbnails and ingested — other
antipsychotics don't work so well. This lunar shell,
penny down wishing well,
craters drag tongue's silt for purchase and
rub the temple wall for relief —
warriors on elephant's back with lances,
dancers with hands pressed for prayer.
Tell time, tell memory of tomorrow's now.
11:47pm.
I could have died many times already,
but I *haven't*, that's the thing.
Flowers, mesmerists of the moonrock garden — behead them —
stroll promenade with whispers
that exhaust the ears of god.

RAIN FELL,
HEAVY, PRECIOUS,
EACH DROPLET A COWRIE SHELL.
LATER WE TRADED IT FOR SILENCE.

'Twas the Night Before COVID

THE LIVING AND THE DEAD

Necromancy's a hard game, especially when the person
you're communicating with isn't dead yet. A fraught art —
like a baptism in a smokehouse, a wedding in a meth lab,
chiselling apart your skeleton to make dice of bone, or
using a border as a skip-rope. She left a crescent moon on
my shoulder, but no one prayed beneath it. He told me that
COVID was punishment for our collective sins, but I left him on *read*.
Through the elliptical lens of a dew drop, we all look
about the same — the living and the dead.

SELF-ISOLATION WASHING MACHINE HEAD

1

Concern yourself with the little things:

Piss on the toilet seat and rust on the showerhead.
A fold-out chair and jalapeño tuna.
A scourer and an NBA podcast.
Instructions on how to wash your hands properly.
Fortune cookies and a message from an ex.
Sour candy and smoke. Friendship.
The foolishness of confessional poetry. The agility of fear.
Meds and panic-bought time.
The mass grave of four-dollar bottles of wine.
A fold-out chair and a can of mango chilli tuna.
A view of a plane tree and the search for god.
Fire in the temple and stone in the gullet.
Piss on the seat and rust on the showerhead.

A regenerative madness.   I have been here before.

2

In a flatblock in Italy, there was a quarantine choir
where neighbours came out on their balconies
and sang in harmony. One of my neighbours
sells ice at pandemic-level prices, lets his too-big
dog shit in my flowerbed and spills McDonald's
thickshakes on the stairs.

The others are okay, though. Nice, even.

One of them waved at me today.

3

I hate everything I've ever written.

I will hate this too.

I speak nonsense most nights —
wander through a maze of pointed fingers
(mostly my own), a circular labyrinth of mirrors.
I close my eyes and survey the landscape of my mistakes,
the Flor de la Mar map, unfolding, a known world
in dying script — scraps missing — lost in a shipwreck
and surviving only in wayfarers' accounts.

But I am not a map of the world.

And fuck it, no more thistle whips
and crowns of thorns — save
self-flagellation for the saints of old,

cos I am no saint.

4

Circular phrases: we often resort to these bite-sized, pop-psych truisms. In some ways they are banal as hell, spoken when there's nothing left to say, when language freezes and the conversation ends. And while it's true *nothing will come of nothing*, Lauryn Hill reminds us that *everything is everything*. Sometimes a circular phrase asserts your selfhood, like Marlo from *The Wire* — *my name is my name*. But Avon, Omar Little and Brother Mouzone would also remind you that *the game is the game*, and never will it change. However, *never say never* — sometimes we hope that the roundabout might straighten out at some point in the future and transform into a road that goes somewhere. But, sometimes, there's nothing more to say. You have to accept this life, as it is, which leads to death and death to new life. *Sorry not sorry — it is what it is —* a bangle made of glass, a snake's fangs clamped down on its own tail.

5

Through all this cuts something else,
wilder even, fecund, the tracery of leaves
            and vegetation dripping with dew.

Charge it to the game, no, to the world —
            a tiny world. A forest
                    grows inside a skull.

I missed the jungle, so I propagated a memory and made one on my windowsill.
Then I ate tom yum.

Lockdown Nocturne

UNMADE

‘Hear the slipping earth, the slipping earth’ OSIP MANDELSTAM

urgent / the searing verge of skin / bones become flexible and augur infinity / surging / fingerprints supernova and nerves become fibre-optic / overlap / two thermal maps / new territory / made / a single, sovereign state / wait / kisses, they fall like prayers / teardrops made of honey / searching / tongue seeks centre / touch magma / magnets flush on / core the wine sap apple / oh, agonising joy / liquid, whiplash love / horizon around the bed an orbital blue /

but the centre cannot hold / things fall apart (again) / and the earth is slipping, and slipping, away

face / unmade / like bed after sex / like grave / oh, futile ecstasy / glitchy utopia constructed so achingly / deepfake of love / of art, promise / try everything, every - fucking - thing, darling one / now try again / cry for the self and the end of possibility / the fever nothing can palliate / she, too, is sifting the signs / a suburb away / a stalemate / what it was / no tumble of bones could tell a different end

BUNÇA BUNÇA MIMPI

THE FISHERMAN STOPPED TRYING TO HUSTLE ME WHEN HE SAW ME BREAKDOWN. HE SAID I WAS ONCE IN LOVE TOO. WHEN SHE BROKE MY HEART I NEARLY KILLED MYSELF. NOW I ONLY SEE HER IN THE FLOWERS OF DREAMS

KILLERNOVA

i suppose we were dead already

(dead to each other, at least),

two dark stars in twin orbit, brutal and balletic,

the furious finale of a never-could-have-been,
          we drew close,

you,   fleet-footed,   smelling of pepper or buckshot,
me,   unsure,
'isn't god supposed to live out here somewhere?' i said,
you laughed, spun, looked over your sunlit shoulder, 'come close, darling one,
let us curate a calamity for the ages, the stars still living are a room of flowers.'
so we lay down together in a garden of zodiacs,   collapsed into each
other's arms and for a moment it felt like the right thing to do —

          — but as soon as flesh met flesh, a stellar explosion, rose gold killernova,
perfect armageddon we sought so recklessly, but the ferocity surprised us both,
didn't it? champagne shockwaves and ribbons of smoke, distrust, blame games
and don't-you-dares, tumblers of whisky shattered into collapsing galaxies,
citadels went tumbling — flares rose, cities fell — circles of friendship //
circles of hell — dreams of rope — it was aborted hopes and uncast votes,
wasn't it? slow-motion tsunami of liquid gold, patterns like ikat cloth on
bloodthirsty royals — what a destructive thing we made, my darling one.

but (space)time heals all   maybe…

or maybe   it just obscures the symptoms…

the shockwaves lost pace and power, tempered with time, subtle as they moved through
space — gamma rays… gravitational waves… waves of hair… the dark matter of our
memories narrowed into a filament, hard to detect as a silken hair stretched between
earth and a distant star — as it twisted sinuous through space, a persuasive melody,
black diamond serpent echoing through / ears / galaxies / keyholes / walls / temples /
souls, it passed through everything in its path, the thermodynamic rumour of our
once-was, containing in its plangent body private jokes and soft-spoken sorries,
the sweet smell of nutmeg jam on pancakes, a slow, startled look under eyelashes
when you finally understood — funny how what starts as never-speak-to-me-again
transforms into: 'the other day i listened to My Sweet Lord and thought of you —
i sat in a rental car and looked out over the mountains, hoping you're well,
wherever you are…'

what was once a killernova,
          just a whisper now,

          a stray earring in a drawer, a button in an ashtray,
                              a sigh / a dream
                              or a dream of a sigh,

a rumour of how chance once choreographed
          two wandering stars in a beautiful dance of death,

          how our unborn child plays peek-a-boo behind kinks in spacetime,
                    waiting to reveal themselves

          130 million light years before we ever even met.

POETRY

They say *write what you know.*

I say *write what you know about what you don't know.*

The universe is a tapestry dyed with squid ink and embroidered with fire opals —
Time is a shadow cast like a net — You are miracle and murder — All good writing is
birthed by risk — To be born is to be complicit.

A rephrasing: *write what you don't know about what you know.*

What monstrous hand, if any, moves the loom?
What silver scales are shed like coins, what gills gasp? Will you ever love me?
What vessel to carry that risk?
Complicit *how*?

This is all to say, yes, write what you know:

write a question.

THE ROLL DOWN

have you ever held a pigeon,

carefully,

like a liver made of glass,

like a carved box holding the bones of a saint?

let it fly.

the deep roller pigeon,

genetically modified acrobat,

favourite of Mike Tyson,

climbs as high as heaven's blue vaults,

tumbling and rolling on the roiling air,

spectacular winged somesaults,

but full of futile fear.

sometimes they can't open their wings

so they backflip

plummet and

crash to earth,

a mine blast of white-grey

a paintball splash of red.

this is called 'the roll down'.

*

he sleeps the sleep

of a carrier pigeon,

magnet heart pea-sized,

twitching for home —

nightmares of mixed signals

and missed landings,

fantasies of the roll down.

The Artists Were Despo

SPIDER
SILK

tough as kevlar / high-grade steel / cloak of kings / fine enough to use as cross-hairs
in a rifle scope / whisper *hold steady* to your prey as you swivel the sights /
but nothing is steady, and no one who is hunter is not also prey /

you cannot force a spider to make silk / it is rebellious and erratic /
you cannot farm it like the mulberry-fed worm / you must be patient

scientists have tried to bottle that lightning / by genetically modifying goats / bleating and
bloated with milk / laced with the same silk / boil that milk, distil it to a bulletproof vest /
a tightrope to dance across with eight pinpoint feet

you like to think you are the spider / or the silk / but maybe you are the milk / or the goat /

or the scientist / dashing brain on desk / to spin false gossamer

ORCHID

I used to think that writing was a matter of life and death. I used to think that a true writer diminishes with each piece of themselves they convert into words and send into the abyss. Not to suggest writing is a selfless or wholly generous act. More likely — deluded, narcissistic, and pathological. The bigger the work, I believed, the smaller you become, withering away, or more like *falling* away, petal by petal, until there is nothing left of you but the hot air of a hot day at the edge of a remote province.
*

My knuckles swell from carving the orchid into this cheap wood,
the glue, the carcinogens in my lungs — inhale art and destruction.

*

I give birth to orchids, sometimes. Butterfly-coloured, they stream
from my navel, up into the pressurised dark of the forest.
They jostle out of my mouth, budding at the corner of my eyes,
tiny then blooming out large, untether, float up, ragged parasols
amongst the knotted skeins and fighting junglecats — yellow, mauve,
pink and white. The most beautiful ones, I cannot claim: they appear
suddenly, perfectly,

birthed, as if,

          by the air itself.

HARRY STYLES AT CHRISTMAS

In the courtyard, mother and son danced for us.

It might have been the penultimate scene of an
indie film (which could somehow afford to
license a global hit song) — slow motion, late evening
sunflare on the lens, mosquitoes and midges
turning watermelon dusk particulate, a thousand
darting sparks of light. Scrappily rehearsed,
sometimes she went left and he went right;
they mimed picking berries with fingers moving
as if playing piano upside-down — he giggled,
embarrassed (she'd bribed him with a video game),
but mostly he kept his eyes on her, intent, gaze broken briefly
when they twirled each other around at the chorus.
As the song strained, alloyed joy, summer almost
became abstraction, but *no*, it was body, and touch,
and lathed sound, enhancement of shadow by light;
it was the shapes of leaves in a garden. Our eyes filled —
those of us without children, who might never have;
chosen as guests in an age with a limit on gatherings
 — there would soon be a day, not so far away,
when son mightn't dance with his mother, not
privately, not publicly, and time, yes *time*,
was playing out so swiftly, burning right down
to the final note of a song about summer and love.

FUCK / BATMAN

AFTER INUA ELLAMS

The truth is parts of us welcomed \ the prophet of oblivion \ its thousand rapturous faces \ the flapping beat of its leathery wings \ its messianic cape \ an accelerant of armageddon \ its balled-up breath plummeting down \ crumpling the traffic jams of our silent screaming \ a weight unknown \ we had always known \ The truth is parts of us secretly rejoiced \ that we could finally drop our masks \ relinquish the facade of civility \ and welcome the end of days \ The wild children wore pasta necklaces \ hunted with sardine cans beaten into shanks \ and streamed toilet paper across the emptied cities \ The grandfathers listening to radio broadcasts \ sanitised their hands with night-brewed moonshine \ and came to different conclusions \ The grandmothers grew parsley and shot Zoom bombers \ There were voices swooping in the skies above the streets \ We sat on our windowsills and drank ink \ singing lockdown nocturnes \ cabin fever-dreaming \ unscrambling our future from a mess of blinding stars \ We looked for patterns and rearranged history \ We made jigsaw pictures of places we might never visit again \ There is Mount Kinabalu and the Tamparuli Bridge \ Here is Semporna with yellow and pink coral \ There are the reefs that will breathe again \ Here are turtles and their quiet hymns \ We grew madder yet clearer headed with each day \ We cried and laughed and cried again \ We chiselled our faces to suit our moods \ and settled on perverse Joker smiles \ We melted all the votive candles we had lit in tribute to our pasts \ and recast them as clear crayons \ to create the myths of our tomorrows

AUTUMN DECIDES

we fall like ginkgo leaves
from the sky.

turn gold   bright lies   make promise prehistoric.

none of this is new

a brilliant reprise along the avenues
dappled with the pattern of our histories.
now memory
elides broken
voices into hallmark wisdom —
you said (i think)
'new beginnings are born from goodbyes.'

we will be swept into dark gutters,
you and i,
where all others evanesce —

glow down to winter,
glow down to silt.

PALEOCHANNEL

I'll let you in on the metaphor early.

Kintsugi: the Japanese art of repairing broken ceramics by filling the cracks with precious metals, to make an object more beautiful than before.

It seems impossible to accept the axiom when he says it with sober-eyed intensity; my sponsor (like another) loves to speak of alchemy and quote Carl Jung — 'the shadow is 90 per cent pure gold.'

In Lahad Datu, on the east coast of Sabah, there are alluvial deposits, once-were rivers called 'paleochannels', where people look for gold. Wikipedia says that paleochannels are of geological importance because they help us understand the 'movement of faults'.

Twelve Steps down to the paleochannel now. Layer cake of shame and revelation, midden of shell and bone, shit and sucked ciggie, unpurged long-drop toilet. I probe like a needle in epidermis, a bin chicken looking for chips — in those rooms at the back of churches, where knees bounce and coffee is sipped from styrofoam. There are others with lithified livers, who hit rock bottom and called out to a god they didn't believe in.

I drank so hard that I shat blood and became a me I hated.

I drank so hard, I was seeking death and found Hell; the drink became the only god I knew, the fool's golden rapture.

I never wore gold growing up. Gold was promised in paradise, I was told, but in this life it is a gaudy and unbecoming adornment. So when I pierced my ears with it and draped myself in chains and brand-name cloth, when I swallowed ribbons of amber, it felt like heresy. But in some Muslim societies, in the 'Golden Age of Islam', gold was used to heal eyes and heart, and in the cauterisation of wounds.

She — I called her my Rose Gold Lover. Maybe even in those words the unfair, fuckboi expectation that a woman should exact golden repair. We only deepened the cracks, it turned out, and made more. When she left, she gave me a Jung quote and a book on Japanese wabi sabi. I threw it in a box. Years later, I found it again. It spoke of beauty in impermanence, transience, and kintsugi. A glowing easter egg, hidden on a page, discarded.

Ninety per cent of the world's gold is created by a kilonova, when two neutron stars collide and create a cataclysmic explosion that sends debris through space and time, shimmering particles that end up compacted into bright treasure, somewhere in the paleochannel beneath my feet.

I am on my knees now. There are other things here — bone beds, crystal skulls, uranium, lignite. Useful but brutal, they burn. But day upon day, I dig on. I seek to pan precious things from shadow: with these hands of clay, this heart that slowly revolves on the potter's wheel.

INVISIBLE MAP

AFTER TOMAS TRANSTRÖMER

Behind every poem, there is an invisible poem.

Behind every map, there is an invisible map.

Behind every you, there is an invisible you.

The search, an impossibility — an imperative.

I WANTED
TO DIE
BUT
NOW I
WANT TO
LIVE

Me and my woodcut guru, Aerick LostControl, Tamparuli Living Arts Centre

Pangrok Sulap in Kota Kinabalu

Aerick and Bam from Pangrok Sulap carving with me

My hosts at Tamparuli Living Arts Centre,
Herman and Christina

Christina working on a massive woodcut with helper Gitom

With my Sabahan mentor and kakak, Yee I-Lann

Pak Jayau, master Dayak Benuaq carver, who I met while travelling up the Mahakam River.

Mancong Longhouse,
Mahakam River,
East Kalimantan

Me and my grandparents at Sepilok Orangutan Park, Sandakan, 1993

pic by Cole Bennetts

Working with Clare Jackson at Megalo Print Studio, Canberra

Working at Curtis Glass Art Studio, Queanbeyan (pic by Cole Bennetts)

Woodcuts in progress (pics by Cole Bennetts)

My first print

ACKNOWLEDGEMENTS

These things are not created alone.

I want to thank Tamparuli Living Arts Centre — Christina, Herman and the fam, Aerick Tan AKA Aerick LostControl, Pangrok Sulap (especially Bam and Rizo), Clare Jackson and Megalo Print Studio, Abdul Abdullah, Jason Phu, Tim Pauszek, Abdi Karya, Helen Musa, Razzaq Bakri, Sabahuddin Senin and my fam in Sabah, Mira Hector, Orangutan Tattoo Studio, Billy Bowring, Caroline Gasteen, Cole Bennetts, Daniel Merriweather, David Stavanger, Bankstown Poetry Slam (especially Sara and Bilal), Emily Bitto, Nam Le, Inua Ellams, Tishani Doshi, Jamal Raslan, Bernice Chauly, Kale Samios, Katie Cunningham, Michael Pedersen, Dominic Hoey, Neldy Jolo, Nadira Ilana, Sang Tukang, Nick Bryant-Smith, Adit Gauchan, Rachel Burke, Rachel Oxenham, Rinaldo Hartanto, Rowan Thomson, Rose Sigang, Jenny Majuine Howard, Tom Horn, Mark Lloyd, Luka Lesson, Sarah McCloskey, Kadi Hughes, Archie Hamilton, Hera Lindsay Bird, Tash Aw, Sophie Cunningham, Elena Gomez, Polly Hemming, Bhenji Ra, Brooke Boney, Sof Ridwan, Simon Cobbold, Laura Jones, Lily Yulianti Farid, Joe Rubbo, Hau Latukefu, Kilifoti Eteuati, Carolina De La Piedra, Tara Wynne and Caitlin Cooper-Trent at Curtis Brown, Nikki Christer, Johannes Jakob (special thanks for your sharp and insightful editing), Rachel Scully and Adam Laszczuk at Penguin Random House Australia, Umbi Gumbi Artist in Residence Program, Civitella Ranieri Foundation, Jon Priadi Barajo, Tiyan Baker, TRACC Turtle Sanctuary, Kae Tempest, Crig AKA Cracko, Nofie, Christos Tsolkias, Simon Armitage, Aaron Kent and Broken Sleep Books. Harriet Schwarzrock and Matt Curtis at Curtis Glass Art Studios. Thanks to Yee I-Lann, Farish Noor and Anthony Reid, to whose work I owe a lot.

And many thanks to you, the reader.

Love and light to you all.

OMAR MUSA

LAY OUT YOUR UNREST

Lightning Source UK Ltd.
Milton Keynes UK
UKHW051955280722
406520UK00003B/60